cheers to life
true to myself

This book is a gift for:

....

From:

....

cheers to life true to myself

A.H. CAMERON STROTHER, PH.D.

Printed in the U.S.A.

Cheers to Life True to Myself

For information about this title or to order other books and/or electronic media, contact the publisher:

First Projection, Inc.
13000 South Tryon Street, Bldg F-132
Charlotte, NC 28278
Phone: 704-243-4779
Fax: 704-843-1498

Library of Congress Control Number: 2011923084
ISBN: 978-0-9832504-1-8

Cover and Interior design: 1106 Design www.1106design.com

For teaching me that
every generation must
pull its wagon further
than the prior generation;

For encouraging me to
advocate for **SELF**
I salute you.

I dedicate these
inspirational passages
to my parents

RONALD AND ETHEL CLARKE.

In Memory

For the love of my father

JESTICE CAMERON

Rest in Peace

2011

Today is the **GIFT** *we must learn to embrace.*

—A.C. JUDGE

Introduction

Each passage in this book presents inspirational definitions for evolutions in life. I refer to these passages as life's reflections. Throughout our lives, we experience defining moments – where life forces us to pause and reflect. Without honesty and reflection, we can never be true to self.

A memorable event occurred when my high school guidance counselor said I should not enroll in college prep classes because my future would not require a college education. Although I disregarded the comments, the imagery of her words has lasted all of my life. Consider that I was a student at legendary Eastside High School (EHS), in Paterson, NJ. The school became famous when Warner Bros. Entertainment, Inc. distributed a biographical film (1989) that was based on true events at EHS. The film was "Lean on Me" and suddenly EHS was cast on the world stage as a dysfunctional educational institution.

For me, life at EHS continues to represent defining moments; reflections of my past and navigation for the future. I challenge you to be true to self and to savor the beauty of the journey.

A.H. CAMERON STROTHER, PH.D.

Journey with me...

Life's experiences are shaped on
Crooked paths that are
Often poorly lit.
Along the way people evolve,
Lessons are harvested and seasons change.
Open your mind. Celebrate the journey.
Imagine deeper meanings of words
Spoken with hushed whispers.
Listen. Explore.
Engage your soul.
Be true to self.

Embrace Life

Oppression is so overwhelming that

In order to move forward

Its virtual barriers must be destroyed.

EMBRACE challenge.

Reflect daily.

Understand life's trials.

Acceptance

To be content with life
You must first
Be at peace
With the private person that
Lives inside you.

Choices

We can **CHOOSE**
To accept unhappiness and
Become intimate with misery or we can
Commit to be aggressive and
Move past pain.
Life is waiting.

Trust

As evening sun sets and darkness appears
I am left with stillness of the air
An occasional breeze
And my deepest thoughts.
Till death do us part,
I am eternally honest with **ME.**
When there are doubts or discontent
TRUST yourself
First.

Adversity

A stepping stone
Along the mountain's rugged path.

Contentment

Forgive errors of others
You are human also
Savor warmth of the moment
Commit to tranquility
Allow yourself to exhale
Practice inner peace
Step forward with confidence.

Inspiration

One who aspires also possesses the ability to

INSPIRE.

Shackles are often created in our past.

We give up power
When we allow **SHACKLES** to
Penetrate the present and future.

When we allow them to destroy
What we have worked to achieve.

Shackles are negative memories.
An invasion of the serenity of life.

Strength

A fine line exists between fear and illusion.
Fear hypnotizes; creates deception.
Fear relaxes positive energy.

Silently we become partners with pain.
We become so familiar with problems
And we convince ourselves that
It's easier to maintain the status quo
Than to be a warrior for change.
Resist the illusion.

Authentic

Exhibit **CONFIDENCE**
Demonstrate **COURAGE**
Endure with **CHARACTER**

Melancholy

To be a prisoner of one's own mind
Yet unable to release from pain,
Ultimately disappointing your inner self
Losing your rightful place in life.

Reflection

Occasionally life makes an abrupt departure
From its customary route.
It shakes our belief systems and
Commands that we
Question ideas we thought were firm.
Those moments of stillness are
Defining moments.
Periods in our lives where everyone else
Seemed to be hurrying past
And yet they really weren't.
We were **STANDING STILL.**
Stillness is a frame of mind.
A reference point.

Balance

There is a difference between
Working to earn a living and
Loving the work you do.
When you attain **BALANCE**
Between the two,
A fulfilling life is created.
Savor the blessing of balance.

Persevere

No one said life would be easy -
So why give in to negativity
When things don't turn out perfectly?
Why give in to despair?

Honesty

For moments when the rawness of life
Forces me to turn away from the gentle wind,
I reflect on what the journey has taught me
And its lessons of perseverance.
Such raw **HONESTY** is deeply humbling,
Necessary and liberating.
It frees me.

Release

As an adult, one must

RELEASE

The inhibitions of their inner child
So life as an adult can be fulfilling.
We all have an inner child
Living within our most
Basic memories.

Exhale

To mold abstract ideas into solid reality

Obstacles must be defeated.

Accept the challenge of life's experiences.

Overcome adversity.

Breathe life to dreams!

Freedom

Trusting my instincts
Honest with self
Proud of my strengths
At peace with my faults
Rejoiced to the sound of my inner voice
Opened the door to peace.

Courage

Occasionally life's journeys
Are so overwhelming that we
Lose sight of who we really are
Until we finally forget.
Illusion becomes reality.
Grasp opportunity to
Turn the page.
Rewrite the story.

Hope

Always precedes success.

Achieve

When someone says you can't achieve or
You're not capable,
Disregard their negativity.
Focus and **ACHIEVE** your goals.

Evolve

Use the past to **EVOLVE** to the future.
Never forget that the fullness of
Life's experiences are
Keys to unlock the future.
Open your mind.
Visualize the key.

The World's Mold

Does not fit me.
It merely complicates a path of success
That is mine to mold and refine.
My destiny to carve out and embrace.

Façade

An invisible mask that penetrates
A beautiful life story.
When you discard the mask
You are empowered to live with purpose.
Abandon the mask.

Enjoy

BEAUTIFUL PRECIOUS MOMENTS

Create awesome memories.

Empowerment

Is all about you,
A state of mind.
A reflection of
Inner peace that is
Celebrated with the universe.

Uniquely you!

Life's Lessons

Life's lessons are learned through trials.

LEARN from them.

Failure re-defined:

Life's precious story.

Swagger

Melodic bodily movements
An expression of one's symphony of life
Exemplified by gyrations occurring in
The evolution of one's journey.
A masterpiece in motion.

Conviction

Opportunity to give birth to a
Past due success.

Exquisite

Hard work with occasional rewards
Never easy
Never handed on a platter
Always an exercise in perseverance.
My life's journey,
A work of art
An incredible **DNA.**

Faith

Refuse to be a victim of your past.
Force the reins to break and
Burn them until they tarnish and fall apart.
Commit to a life of purpose
Guided by **FAITH.**

Move forward.

Imagine

DREAM
BELIEVE
ACHIEVE

Embrace a new journey.

Tranquility

Never forgetting yesterday's lessons but
Refocusing my mind so I can see.
Even though my heart fills with emotion
So much is blurred.
Never forgetting the depth of sorrow
Yet aware that trials are only here for a season;
As sure as sorrow deepens
It will also dim with time.
Leaving this moment
Ready to start a new day.
Periods of sadness are temporary passages
Through the seasons of life.
When they have passed, **MOVEMENT** will
Take over and the view will be clear.

Confidence

Achieve success
With the **CONFIDENCE** that you are
Capable and uniquely designed to
Live your dream.

New Beginnings

While others may cast stones and
Find fault with my choices,
I refuse to allow them
Space to crowd my life.
Yes, I am passionate about
Freedom of movement and the
Dawn of **NEW BEGINNINGS**.

Meditation

To question is the nature of a
Child's imagination.
But what about the adult mind that's closed
To free forms of imagination?
"How did I get to this place,
In this life that I call my own?"
"What decisions have led me here?"
With humble convictions
One must be able to answer these questions.

Passion

Giving more deeply than
I thought
I was capable of.

Coffee Talk

It was just a little coffee talk but it made me
Stop in my tracks.
Small hard cover book
Light in weight. Tan in color.
Not so glamorous
But with words so moving.
Heavy in substance
COFFEE TALK never seemed
So interesting, so vogue,
So compelling. So much about me.
Maybe it wasn't just coffee talk after all.

Peace

With confidence, I share these passages
And am hopeful that you will be
Inspired and encouraged
By these words.
With introspection and faith
I encourage you to be true to self
And to live with purpose
Cheers to life.

PEACE

Notes

Illustrations used in the text were Flowers, Bees, and Hummingbirds. Flowers provide nectar so that Bees and Hummingbirds reproduce and continue to thrive.

In some cultures Bees symbolize wisdom, order, soul, grace, balance, self-transformation, and community.

Hummingbirds symbolize pure love, joy, optimism, devotion, wonder, and beauty. Hummingbirds are regarded as lights in the darkness and represent celebration of life.

In a world that often seems full of adversity, A.H. Cameron Strother, Ph.D. introduces *Cheers to Life–True to Myself,* an inspirational book that celebrates life experiences as an evolving journey. With a refreshing approach, A.H. Cameron Strother uses thought-provoking word passages to illustrate that when we reflect on life's lessons and are honest with our innermost feelings, we are empowered to live with purpose. This book guides your journey. You will know when it is time to pause and reflect.

Inspirational words are profound when they whisper to your soul and warm your heart; when you feel at peace with the past and look forward to the future with positive energy. The beauty of the experience lies in how well we understand life's lessons. Savor the journey.

A.H. Cameron Strother, Ph.D. received a doctoral degree from Capella University, a Master of Arts degree from Webster University, and a Bachelor of Science degree from South Carolina State University. She has worked in manufacturing for many years and is the President of TruBlend Café, a company that distributes gourmet Arabica coffee beans from locales such as Costa Rica, Rwanda, Zimbabwe, Ethiopia, and Brazil. Dr. Cameron Strother lives in North Carolina and has published in the Journal of International Business. She loves animals and has two rescue cats named Buddy and Smokey-Blue. She is married and has two children.

Please contact the author at acstrother@trublendcafe.com

To learn more about TruBlend Café:

www.trublendcafe.com